T0365946

Daily
Text
Messages
of
Encouragement

WLA
ggma

WESTBOW®
PRESS
A DIVISION OF THOMAS NELSON
& ZONDERVAN

WestBow Press books may be ordered through booksellers or by contacting:

WestBow Press
A Division of Thomas Nelson & Zondervan
1663 Liberty Drive
Bloomington, IN 47403
www.westbowpress.com
1 (866) 928-1240

ISBN: 978-1-4908-8497-4 (sc)
ISBN: 978-1-4908-8498-1 (hc)
ISBN: 978-1-4908-8496-7 (e)

Library of Congress Control Number: 2015909815

Print information available on the last page.

WestBow Press rev. date: 6/29/2015

To _____

From _____

Date _____

Acknowledgements

TO GOD BE ALL THE GLORY

My Deepest Appreciation to
Katie Michaelson for Graphic Design
and Special Thanks to Heather Ingram
and Rachelle Heverly.

Gloria Laine

Dedication

This is Dedicated to my
Mother and Daddy,
who are a never ending
Song in my Heart of
Unwavering Faith,
Love and Encouragement.

And
To Kathleen, Rictor, Heather,
Brennan, Andrew, Travis,
Steve, Linsey, Shaelen,
Sebastian and Richard,
whom I Cherish more than
Life itself, for they are my
Reason for being here.

Introduction

In these busy days, it may be difficult to keep in touch with those we love, especially the young people. Although they don't realize it, they desperately need words of wisdom and the unconditional, loving affirmation we can give them. When Brennan, my oldest Great Grandson started High School, he received his first cell phone. There wasn't enough time in the morning to wish him a happy day, so I got the idea of sending him a happy text message every morning before he went to school. Sometimes, I would send interesting facts, and sometimes, jokes. I just wanted him to know I was thinking of him and sending loving thoughts his way. When Andrew, my second Great Grandson started High School, and received his cell phone, I began sending messages to him too.

Soon, some of Brennan and Andrew's Friends asked to receive the daily messages also. That is how this book came about. There are Moms and Dads, Grandmas, Grandpas, Aunts, Uncles, and caring Friends who want to send Loving Thoughts of Encouragement to their young people, but don't know what to say or how to say it. This is a book of suggestions of how to reach out and show them you Love them, Believe in them, and Value them. And frankly, not only teenagers need to hear that. We All Do. Believe it or not, you will feel so good inside when you encourage others. Just try it. See if it works for you as it has for me.

WLA

(With Love Always)

ggma

(Great Gramma)

A Personal Message

Every message comes with my
sincerest Prayer that it will
touch your Heart and Life
and Encourage You to Become
the Very Best Person YOU can be,
so you can Help Others do the same.
    May GOD'S Love Guide You
    Every Day of Your Life.
                    WLA
                    ggma

Your LIFE Can Make A Difference
One Little Star Can
Light Up The Night.
One Helping Hand Can
Make Things Right.
One Friendly Smile Can
Change a Sad Mood.
One Quiet Voice Can
Whisper the Truth.

YOU are Unique and
Wonderfully made. There
is no one exactly like you
in the Whole World.
YOU ARE A TREASURE
OF GREAT VALUE.

–WLA
ggma

"LIFE is like a mirror.
If You Smile into it,
It will Smile back at You."
  -Old Chinese Proverb
KEEP SMILING AND
WORKING ON
THE GOOD LIFE.

–WLA
ggma

_____

_____

_____

YOU are a Success Story
in progress and you are
writing an Exciting chapter
right now. It's Awesome to
be Young, Good-Looking
and Smart too.

–WLA
ggma

Treat each day as a Special Gift. Choose to LIVE Your Life with a Capital "L." Celebrate LIFE Every Day! Inspire Others to do the same.

–WLA
ggma

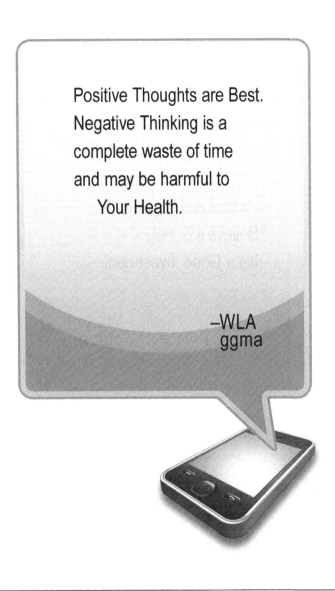

Positive Thoughts are Best.
Negative Thinking is a
complete waste of time
and may be harmful to
Your Health.

–WLA
ggma

YOU can buy a CLOCK
but you can't buy TIME.
Every moment is PRICELESS.
Spend Your Time being
   Helpful and Kind.
   Believe it or not,
   It's a Good Investment.

–WLA
ggma

LIFE is Not a Competition
to be Better than Anyone
or Get More Stuff. It is
about being Morally
Responsible and Respectful
of Yourself and Others.

–WLA
ggma

_____

_____

_____

COMPASSION AND HOPE
Do Not require cash or coupons.
Spread them around FREELY
and You Will Be Wealthy
Beyond Measure.

–WLA
ggma

KNOWLEDGE is Proud that it Knows so much. WISDOM is Humble because it knows there is so much MORE TO LEARN.

–WLA ggma

Challenges are not
meant to paralyze you.
They are meant to stretch
you and help you Discover
How to Become
YOUR VERY BEST SELF.

–WLA
ggma

"If you LISTEN to instruction to improve YOUR LIFE, You will LIVE among the WISE and GAIN UNDERSTANDING."

–WLA
ggma

Your Success depends 10% on what happens to you and 90% how you respond to it. Stay Calm with positive thoughts and CONFIDENCE IN YOURSELF.

–WLA
ggma

_____

_____

_____

Do you sing in the shower?
You Should! Start the day
with a Song. Make it Your
Day. Let the world know
you are Alive and Well
and Ready to Take Charge.

–WLA
ggma

Don't be afraid to take a
Risk by doing something
Good. If Michelangelo
had been afraid, he would
have painted the floor
instead of the ceiling.

–WLA
ggma

Even if you are on the Right
Track, you will be run over
if you just sit there.
Keep Moving Forward.
Don't Look Back.
Exciting Things are Ahead.

–WLA
ggma

YOU are BRAVER than you think you are. You have the Courage to face your fears and REACH OUT for Your Dreams. I Believe in YOU. Do You Believe in YOU?

–WLA
ggma

BELIEVING is the Ignition Switch that gets you OFF the Launch Pad and Into the Galaxy called Success.

–WLA ggma

_____

_____

_____

Right is Right even if
Everyone is Against it.
Wrong is wrong even if
Everyone is For it.
Listen to the Whisper
    Of Your Heart.

–WLA
ggma

Doubt and Fear are
Robbers. They steal
Your Confidence
And Motivation.
FIGHT BACK!
Chase them away.
Get a New Plan of Action.
BE BRAVE AND STRONG!
–WLA
ggma

Loving Kindness Grows
Wherever You Plant it.
It is Exciting to see how
much it Multiplies.
Plant some Today
and Watch what happens.

–WLA
ggma

STOP Judging and Comparing Yourself to Others. You have a Brilliant Mind with Talents and Skills like no one else. Let Yourself Grow to Become Who YOU are meant to be.

–WLA ggma

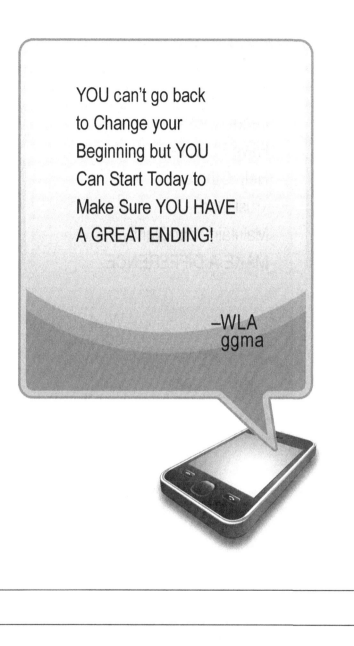

Think. Dream.
Learn Constantly.
Have Patience.
Help Others.
Trust God.
Maintain Your Dignity.
MAKE A DIFFERENCE.

–WLA
ggma

_____

_____

_____

*An eagle cannot rest in a
Sparrow's nest. Each one
is important, but they
have different Abilities.
Are you like an Eagle or
a Sparrow? Will You Fly
to the Mountaintop, or
Nestle in the Treetops?*

No One can diminish you
unless you let them.
You know who you are
and where you are going.
Keep a Good Self Image
In Your Heart

–WLA
ggma

Build your house with a Strong Foundation. Use the Best Materials you can find. It will be Your Shelter during the storms. DO THE SAME WITH YOUR LIFE.

–WLA
ggma

_____

_____

_____

Your Cheerful Outlook
is like a Sunny Day.
It makes Everyone
around You Feel
Happy To Be Alive.

–WLA
ggma

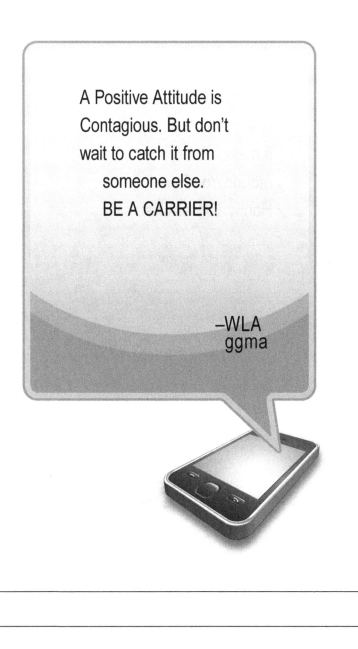

"WORRY often gives a
very SMALL thing a
very BIG shadow."
-Swedish Proverb
(Worry doesn't take away
tomorrow's troubles, It
takes away Today's Peace.)

–WLA
ggma

_____

_____

_____

Courage isn't always a
Lion's Roar. Sometimes
Your Heart whispers,
"You don't need the voice
of a Lion. YOU have the
HEART OF A CHAMPION."

–WLA
ggma

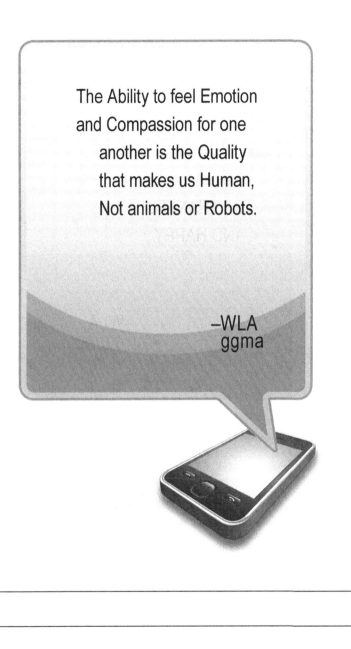

YOU are a truly Amazing
Individual. Just THINK
about how Perfectly You
are put together.
BE THANKFUL
AND HAPPY.

–WLA
ggma

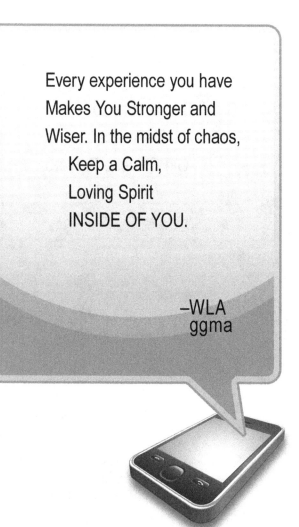

Every experience you have
Makes You Stronger and
Wiser. In the midst of chaos,
  Keep a Calm,
  Loving Spirit
INSIDE OF YOU.

–WLA
ggma

YOU are an Inspiration to Others in what you Say and Do. Be a Leader, not a Follower. Make Sure You Are Going In The Right Direction.

–WLA ggma

Enjoy the Little Things
in Your Life. For one day
you may look back and
realize they were
    The Big Things
    In Your Life.

–WLA
ggma

NO ACT OF KINDNESS
is ever Wasted, no matter
how big or how small.
"Kindness is a Language
that even the Deaf can hear
and the Blind can see."
-Mark Twain

–WLA
ggma

There's nothing wrong with
People possessing Riches.
The danger arises when
Riches Possess the People.
IT DEPENDS ON
YOUR PRIORITIES.

–WLA
ggma

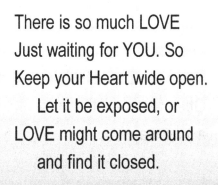

There is so much LOVE
Just waiting for YOU. So
Keep your Heart wide open.
Let it be exposed, or
LOVE might come around
and find it closed.

–WLA
ggma

ADVICE is like Snow;
The softer it falls,
The more Beautiful it is.
Often times a little goes
a long way.

–WLA
ggma

Knowledge is One of
the Great Treasures in
Your Life. You can Always
Use it; Keep it with You
everywhere you go and
NO ONE can ever
take if from YOU.

—WLA
ggma

One of our biggest mistakes is being afraid we will make one. Keep Trying. Everyone makes mistakes. LEARN from them and You will Do Better the next time.

–WLA ggma

Just when a caterpillar thinks its
struggles have all been in vain and
its World is coming to an end,
It Becomes a Beautiful Butterfly.
THE PERFECT PLAN.

-WLA
ggma

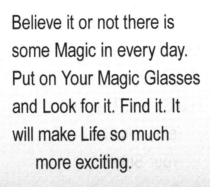

Believe it or not there is
some Magic in every day.
Put on Your Magic Glasses
and Look for it. Find it. It
will make Life so much
more exciting.

–WLA
ggma

A Friend is like a Flower:
Beautiful when standing
alone, but way more Fun
in a Bunch. Thanks for
letting me be in
Your Bunch.

–WLA
ggma

As long as You Live, keep Learning how to LIVE WELL. Each day, Nourish your Inside Self with Love and Confidence and Your Outside Self Will Surely Thrive.

–WLA
ggma

ERASE the word "boring" from your vocabulary and Your Life. USE Your Incredibly Creative Mind to Make This World A Better Place. YES YOU CAN ! ! !

–WLA ggma

Start each day with Great Expectations. Wake Up and say, "Hello New Day. Can't wait to see what exciting things will happen today."

–WLA ggma

LIFE is a Mysterious, Wonderful Present that YOU unwrap One Day At A Time. What will you do with Your Gift Today?

–WLA
ggma

For the Hopeful, Ambitious People, A Week holds Seven Exciting, Busy Days. For the Lazy, Indifferent People it holds many long, worthless, nonproductive hours.

–WLAggma

When YOU want to FIND
the Answers in LIFE,
YOU must Actively Search
for them. Rarely, if ever,
do they fall in your lap.

–WLA
ggma

TRUE STORY: Years ago,
before the Berlin Wall came
down, some East Berliners
dumped truck-loads of
garbage over the wall
into West Berlin. In return,
the West Berliners brought
bread, fruit, canned food
and stacked it neatly at the
East Gate with a sign on top,
"EACH GIVES WHAT HE HAS.'

Don't ever hesitate to say the smallest Word of Encouragement to someone. It may Change THEIR LIFE FOREVER AND YOURS TOO.

–WLA
ggma

Although you may not
realize it, when you let
Your Own Light Shine,
You Show Others how
to do the same. So Be
A Shining Example Of
All Good things.

–WLA
ggma

Instead of measuring yourself by any past mistakes you may have made, VALUE YOURSELF for the Lives You Touch with Loving Kindness Every Day.

–WLA
ggma

Hey, Are You that Handsome Guy (Gorgeous Girl) with the Sparkling Eyes and Friendly Smile who makes Others feel Happy to be alive?
YES YOU ARE!

–WLA ggma

In the battle between
Good and Evil,
COURAGE MUST BE
STRONGER THAN FEAR.
The Quality of Your Life
Depends On It.

—WLA
ggma

How Quiet the morning would be if only the Birds who sang Best were allowed to sing. Fill the World with Your Own Special music. IT WILL BE GREAT!

–WLA ggma

You don't have to be
"Super Human" to be
an Encourager. Your
Friendly Smile and
Kind Words can make
Someone FEEL
"SUPER HUMAN."

–WLA
ggma

YOU probably won't Trip
over a Big Mountain but
You can Stumble on a
Small Stone in your Path.
Watch where you Walk
and soon You Will
Reach Your Mountaintop.

–WLA
ggma

Sometimes LIFE just isn't fair, but it's still Good. It can't be Disneyland every day. Some days it is a quiet walk on a lonely street, but soon that WILL CHANGE.

–WLA
ggma

If You really want to Change it's Up To You! The Time is NOW. TODAY! Let's see that "I CAN DO IT SMILE." Aw, You are such a Cutie-patootie.

–WLA
ggma

When everything seems to be going wrong, STOP for just one moment. THINK of One Good Thing that has happened recently. Now, don't You Feel Better?

–WLA ggma

Make Your Heart a refuge
"Where never is heard a
discouraging word." Be
Uplifting to Everyone,
Including Yourself.

–WLA
ggma

To Gain Wisdom, Develop
a Passion for READING,
LISTENING and THINKING.
(Laughter, Adventure and
Kindness will also make
Your Life Memorable.)

–WLA
ggma

A Word of Encouragement
when something has failed
is Worth MORE than a TON
of PRAISE after something
has been Successful.

–WLA
ggma

Courtesy and Manners are Appreciated and Admired by Everyone. The Respect You Show Others reflects how much Respect You Have for Yourself.

—WLA
ggma

If You Acknowledge them
and LEARN from them,
the mistakes you made
yesterday will help you
to be Brave, Strong and
SMARTER - Tomorrow.

–WLA
ggma

_____

_____

_____

YOU can't push the Waves
to shore any faster than
the Ocean brings them in.
Their Timing is Perfect.
Try to Find the Perfect
TEMPO FOR YOUR LIFE.

–WLA
ggma

A Leader sees Life as it
Should Be and Can Be.
The World says,
"I have to See it
to Believe it."
A Good Leader says,
"Let's Believe it
until We See it."

−WLA
ggma

Desire, Discipline and Determination are Important Bridges between Dreams, Goals and Accomplishments. Keep Working on those Bridges. YOU'LL MAKE IT!

–WLA
ggma

Dust off that Gorgeous Smile
hiding on Your Inner Shelf.
You don't use it enough.
Dress up Your Face.
Show the World
YOUR VERY BEST SELF.

–WLA
ggma

WORRY is the darkroom
where negatives develop.
Don't waste your Incredible
Creative Imagination there.
THINK! Use Your Best
Judgment and GO FOR IT!

–WLA
ggma

In the Great Orchestra of
LIFE, YOU have a Fine
Instrument to Play and
a Special Song only
YOU CAN SING.
Fill the World with Your
Own Beautiful Music.

–WLA
ggma

Laughter is a Great "Shock
Absorber" for the pot holes
in Your Highway of Life.
Try to find an amusing side
of Your most annoying
problems and L O L.

Treat Others as they are and they will remain the same. Treat Them as They COULD BE and They Will Become WHO THEY SHOULD BE.

–WLA ggma

Thought du jour: "What
Good Deeds can I Do Today?"
When You help someone
climb up the Mountain,
You reach the Top as well.
See how that works?

–WLA
ggma

Hey, did you know you are multi-lingual? A Smile means the same thing in every language, even Sign Language and Body Language. YOU ARE SO AWESOME.

–WLA
ggma

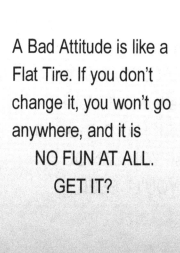

A Bad Attitude is like a Flat Tire. If you don't change it, you won't go anywhere, and it is NO FUN AT ALL. GET IT?

—WLA ggma

THINK about Your
Amazing Talents,
NOT Your flaws.
THINK about
Becoming Your
Very Best Self.
NOW THAT'S
SUCCESS ! !

—WLA
ggma

The Electric Co. brings
power to your home.
YOU turn it ON to USE it.
A Higher Power Offers
Guidance to Your Heart.
YOU BELIEVE IT
TO RECEIVE IT.

–WLA
ggma

The Eagle who Soars High on the Breezes does not worry about crossing the wild, raging Rivers. Your Breezes may be Your Faith, Your Dreams, Your Choices.

–WLA
ggma

When You face a tough challenge, Stretch Up to Your Tallest, Pull Your Shoulders Back, Look Up and Shout, "I was Born to do this and I WILL DO IT."

–WLA
ggma

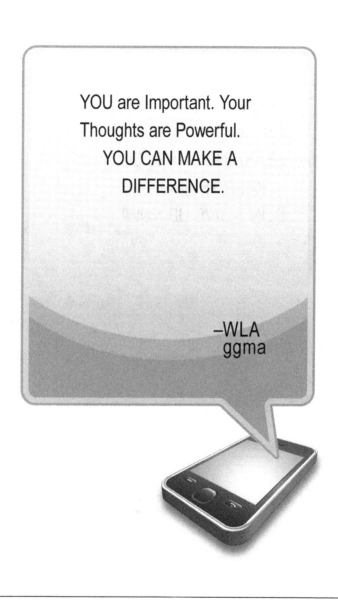

There will be some Storms
in Your Life. Stay Calm.
Keep Your Eyes On Your
Goals. Remember,
    You are Learning
To Sail Your Own Ship.

—WLA
ggma

It doesn't matter how slowly you go TOWARD Your Goals, as long as you DON'T STOP. Keep Moving in the direction of Your Dreams.

–WLA ggma

_____

_____

_____

Be like a Sponge. Absorb all the Knowledge, Beauty and Love that surround you. Then Squeeze a little out on Everyone You Meet.

–WLA ggma

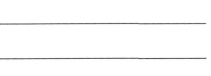

YOU have a Brilliant Mind.
Nourish it. Cherish it.
Use it to advance your
Dreams and Plans for
A Beautiful Life.

—WLA
ggma

Kind Words are like Honey.
They taste good and make
You Happy and Healthy
At the Same Time.

–WLA
ggma

You Are Loved!
Let this knowledge
settle into Your Heart
and give you the
Freedom to Sing,
Dance, Laugh,
Love and Be Loved.

–WLA
ggma

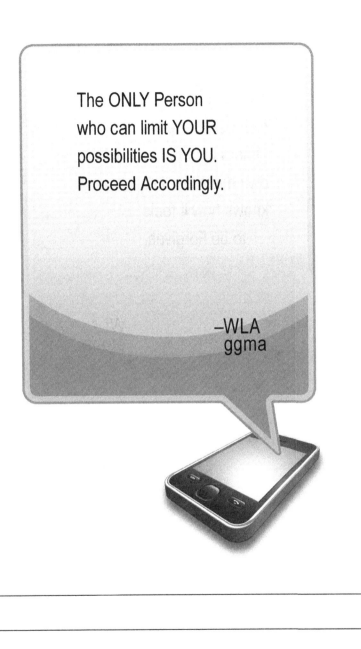

A Loving Heart can
overlook the faults of
Others for it remembers its
own mistakes and
knows how it feels
to be Forgiven.

–WLA
ggma

Be Careful how you Live.
There are those who are
watching You even when
it appears they aren't
listening to you.

–WLA
ggma

When You Learn to appreciate the simple things in Life, You will discover that you are surrounded by endless possibilities wearing Ordinary clothes.

—WLA
ggma

D. P. B. D.
DREAM IT.
PLAN IT.
BELIEVE IT.
DO IT.
YOU ARE AWESOME!

–WLA
ggma

A tiny Seed must have
Time, some rain and
the Sun's Energy to
Grow and Bloom. YOU
have the Time and
Power inside of You to
Grow and Become the
Very Best You Can Be.

–WLA
ggma

WORK HARD and
Become a Leader for
Others to Follow.
Don't become a slave to
your own idleness.
BE AN INSPIRATION
TO THOSE AROUND YOU.

–WLA
ggma

Which TENT do you want
to Live in, ConTENT or
DisconTENT? ConTENT
is where the Grateful
And Happy People THRIVE!
DisconTENT is where the
envious and miserable
Barely Survive.
YOU GET TO CHOOSE!

One of the Best Exercises for
Your Heart is
Reaching Out and
Lifting SOMEONE UP.

–WLA
ggma

Write your disappointments in the Sand at low tide. Chisel your Accomplishments in Stone with Humble Gratitude.

–WLA ggma

Whether it is a chore you hate, a project you Love or a Secret Desire, Finishing is Better than Starting and More Rewarding too.
It's a Great Feeling.

–WLA
ggma

The Love of Family and
Friends; the Beauty of
Nature; the Value of
Being Honest, Loving,
Helpful and Kind;
THINK ON THESE THINGS
and BE THANKFUL.

–WLA
ggma

Your possessions DO NOT determine who you really are. You Build your True Character with the Thoughts and Choices YOU make each day.

–WLA
ggma

Just when you think Life is
so predictable, something
completely unexpected and
wonderful happens.
GET READY !
You don't want to miss it.

–WLA
ggma

Encouragement is Oxygen
for the SOUL. Give some to
Everyone you meet. Try to
show each person how
important they really are
to you and to the World.

–WLA
ggma

There is a Mountain named Success. The Road is steep and uphill all the way, but the VIEW at the TOP is worth it. Don't stop until YOU SEE IT.

–WLA
ggma

The shortest distance between two Strangers is a Friendly Smile and a Cheery "Hello."

–WLA ggma

YOU deserve a Big Pat
on the back for Not
giving up; for keeping
Your Dreams alive AND
for wearing that
Wonderful Smile.

–WLA
ggma

Time and Energy are limited necessities and should be used Wisely. There is a Time to Work and a Time to Play. Strive for Balance in Your Life.

–WLA
ggma

Intelligent People desire to LEARN. Science has proven that the more you know, the more you want to know and the more You Need To Know.

–WLA ggma

The Way to GAIN the
Most from LIVING
is NOT in Keeping,
but in GIVING!

–WLA
ggma

YOU are looking so fine today.
People will think You are
Royalty. Just Smile and
give them a Royal Wave.
LIFE IS GRAND, ISN'T IT?

–WLA
ggma

GENIUS is the Gold in Your Mine. Talent and Skill are the Miners who work hard to Bring it Out. KEEP DIGGING. YOU CAN BECOME GOLDEN!

−WLA ggma

At every Age Your Life
should be moving Forward.
A Drifting Boat doesn't
GO ANYWHERE.
Don't Lose Sight of
YOUR GOALS.

–WLA
ggma

A Beautiful Relationship
requires the same attention
to detail as a Great Artist
gives to each one of his
Magnificent Paintings.

–WLA
ggma

_____

_____

_____

YOU and I can make the World A Better Place, one person at a time. Let's Focus on **BUILDING PEOPLE UP,** Instead of Tearing Them Down.

—WLA ggma

To Know the Joy of Living;
Get Ready, Get Set, BEGIN.
You have to Play the Game
Before You Can Win.
Don't Give Up!
Finishing is the Reward.

–WLA
ggma

Get Excited About Life.
Be Interested & Interesting.
Be Stimulated & Stimulating.
REMEMBER, YOU ARE ONE
OF THE BEAUTIFUL PEOPLE.

–WLA
ggma

"Guard Your Heart with all diligence, for out of it Flows the Passion and Motivation for Your Life."

–WLA
ggma

Visualize a Powerful Box
of Crayons inside your
Head. Each morning You
can COLOR Yourself
Happy, Sad, Glad of Mad.
Which Color will YOU
CHOOSE TODAY?

–WLA
ggma

Remembering the
GOOD TIMES is the
GLUE that will HOLD
YOU together when
the Rough Times
make you feel like
you are falling apart.

–WLA
ggma

Do You have a Secret Desire living in your Heart? Treasure it like a Dear Friend. Keep it Strong and Bright as a Guiding Light.

–WLA
ggma

We Learn to Live
   By Living.
We Learn to Love
   By Loving.
We Learn to Forgive
   By Forgiving.
We Learn to Work
   By Working.
We Learn to Believe
   By Believing.
We Learn to Win
BY NEVER GIVING UP!

One Candle loses none
of its OWN Radiance
when Lighting another
Candle. In fact there is
Twice as much Light.
And so it is with
Encouragement.

–WLA
ggma

Just THINK of all the
Great Things about
Yourself. You have so
many Excellent Qualities
and You Are Getting
Better Every Day.
WOOHOO FOR YOU!

–WLA
ggma

Your Mission today, if
you choose to accept it,
is "Be Helpful and Kind
    To everyone."
IT IS NOT IMPOSSIBLE.
This message will
self-destruct in
5 seconds...4...3...2...
                    –WLA
                     ggma

_____

_____

_____

I Dare You to look in the
Mirror to SEE the Change in
your face when you SMILE.
Did you SEE the lights
come ON in your Eyes?
I Love To See You Smile!

–WLA
ggma

SUCCESS happens when
Good Preparation catches
up to Opportunity. THINK
about that and then
DO Something about it.

–WLA
ggma

Why don't Volunteers get paid? Is it because they are worthless? NO. It's because they are PRICELESS. Their Reward is stored in their Heart Forever.

—WLA ggma

BELIEVE IN YOURSELF.
Start Working & Planning
how YOU can Build A
Better World for Others
and Yourself. IT WILL
TOTALLY BE WORTH
THE EFFORT.

—WLA
ggma

Make your Dreams and Goals Flexible. There may be more exciting possibilities than you can imagine right now. Keep Your Heart Right and Your Eyes Open.

—WLA
ggma

YOU have the Amazing
Ability to make a
Significant Contribution
to the World around you.
YOU CAN MAKE A
   DIFFERENCE.
   START TODAY.

   –WLA
   ggma

Some days it feels like everything is going against you. Remember, an Airplane takes off AGAINST the Wind.
LET THOSE WINDS LIFT YOUR WINGS!

–WLA
ggma

YOU are Friendly,
Courteous, Helpful,
Kind, Respectful,
Encouraging, Reliable,
Generous, Funny and
SMART. ALL THAT AND
GOOD LOOKING TOO.

–WLA
ggma

All You have Learned so far is Important. Don't put your Brain on auto-pilot now. Exercise it. Keep it Healthy and Strong so it will WORK FOR YOU a long time.

–WLA
ggma

YOU have what it takes to get all the GOOD THINGS IN LIFE. So Reach Out and Grab That GOLD RING.
IT'S YOURS!
(Leave the brass ring for someone else.)

–WLA
ggma

Do you think much about your Future? You know, Dream of all the things you would like to do in Life. Maybe you should Make a Bucket List.

–WLA
ggma

Okay. Let's Go! It's Time
to tackle that project you
have been dreading. Once
you start you will find it
is easier than you thought
and even Fun, maybe.

–WLA
ggma

_____

_____

_____

FOCUS on Your Strengths
NOT your faults. Forgive
yourself if you make a
mistake. Nobody's
Perfect. YOU ALWAYS
GET ANOTHER CHANCE.

—WLA
ggma

MIRACLES are all around you.
Open the Eyes of Your Heart
and recognize them.
ENJOY THEM AND
BE GRATEFUL.

—WLA
ggma

"You make a Living with
what you get. You make
a LIFE with what you GIVE."
-Sir Winston Churchill

–WLA
ggma

SUCCESS is not only
defined by what you
Accomplish in your
Lifetime, but the
obstacles you have
to OVERCOME and
the People You Help
Along The Way.

–WLA
ggma

You cannot control the Wind but you can adjust your sails to take advantage of it. Then IT WILL HELP YOU GO WHEREVER YOU WANT TO GO.

–WLA ggma

You have
GREATNESS
Inside of You.
Welcome it.
Work with it.
WATCH IT
GROW ! !

—WLA
ggma

One Way to make the
World a Better Place is:
Show Others they are
Important and you really
Care about them. Try it!
See if it works.

–WLA
ggma

Have I told you lately
that I think YOU are
Terrific, Outstanding,
Super Wonderful,
Really Cute and
Brilliant too?
YOU ARE ALL
THAT AND MORE!

–WLA
ggma

HOPE is that thing that GLOWS DEEP IN YOUR SOUL like a burning ember. Never let it die out or be extinguished.

–WLA
ggma

Did Someone do a Kind
Deed for you today?
   Pass It On.
Was a Friendly Smile
sent your way?
   Pass It On.
Be sure to Pass Along
   the "Good Stuff"
and Throw Away the
   "Bad Stuff."

You just never know
how GREAT you can be
or how much you can
accomplish in Life.
Keep Working and
Trying. Nothing
Worthwhile is ever
QUICK OR EASY.

–WLA
ggma

Remember, when you feel like you are at the END of one thing, You are actually at the BEGINNING of many exciting and new opportunities.
SO GET GOING!

–WLA
ggma

TROUBLE always comes with a nugget of Gold in her hand. It may be large or very small and usually hidden from view.

FIND IT.
CLAIM IT.
USE IT FOR GOOD.

−WLA
ggma

"When You need to
MOVE a Mountain,
START by carrying
away the Small Stones."
-Old Chinese Proverb

–WLA
ggma

YOUR LIFE will be more
meaningful when you
focus on the GOOD you
can do for OTHERS instead
of what They can do For You.

–WLA
ggma

The Poor Man is NOT HE who has No Money. He is the Man who has NO Hopes and Dreams. May YOU become RICH in PURPOSE and VISION for a Bright Future.

–WLA ggma

HELPING OTHERS has its
own REWARDS and Expects
Nothing in return.
TRY IT.
You'll like it.
I guarantee it.

–WLA
ggma

***EXTRA...EXTRA...
READ ALL ABOUT IT ***
95% OF everything you
    worry about,
NEVER HAPPENS.
You can handle the
other 5% NO PROBLEM.

–WLA
ggma

Laughter has great
Healing Qualities. It
Relaxes the Tension
in Your Heart and
Shrinks the Fear in
your Mind. Have a
Good Laugh.
See if it works.

–WLA
ggma

When you spill a lot
of Sunshine on those
around you, it splashes
all over You too.
(pssst...YOUR "SHINE"
will be even more
powerful when it's cloudy.)

–WLA
ggma

Some of the Brightest
Stars can only be seen
during the Darkest Nights.
LOOK for them. They
are Twinkling there
FOR YOU bringing
HOPE for Tomorrow.

–WLA
ggma

You don't have to be
Perfect to be Amazing.
You have a Good Heart
and a Good Mind.
USE THEM TO THE
BEST OF YOUR ABILITY.

–WLA
ggma

FREEDOM does NOT give
You the Right to do whatever
you want to do. It Gives YOU
the Opportunity to become
the Very Best Person You
Can Possibly Be.

–WLA
ggma

THANKFULNESS is
a Super Highway to
Happiness. Find some
things to be Thankful
for today. They are all
around you.
I'm Thankful For You.

–WLA
ggma

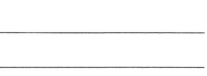

_____

_____

_____

SET LOFTY GOALS.
   AIM HIGH.
SHOOT FOR THE MOON.
EVEN IF YOU MISS,
   YOU WILL LAND
AMONG THE STARS.

–WLA
ggma

At times Your Journey
may not be easy or even
pleasant, but HOLD ON!
There is a ticket on the
"HAPPILY EVER AFTER"
TRAIN WAITING FOR YOU.

–WLA
ggma

There are times when
Your Smile can be the
Best Medicine for an
Aching Heart. Go ahead.
HEAL SOMEONE TODAY.

–WLA
ggma

YOU ARE AN ORIGINAL!
The beating of Your Heart
has Purpose and Your
Actions are Important.
Your Life and what you
do with it Today
MATTERS FOREVER.

–WLA
ggma

"We Grow Too Soon Old,
And Too Late Smart."
        -Old Dutch Proverb
Don't ever stop Learning
and Trying to be Your
    VERY BEST SELF.

                    –WLA
                    ggma

Good face to face
Conversations are as
stimulating as black
coffee. They ignite the
Energy for Creative
Thought and Action.
That's a Good Thing!

–WLA
ggma

You have an Exciting
Journey ahead of you.
"If you want to know the
Road Ahead, ASK someone
who has traveled it."
                    -Old Chinese Proverb

                                    –WLA
                                    ggma

_____

_____

_____

Are you taking lessons
or reading a book on
"How To Become More
Charming and Lovable."
IT'S WORKING

—WLA
ggma

Friendship is One of the Greatest Gifts you can Give or Receive. But Friends are like balloons. If you don't hold on to them, they may fly away.

–WLA
ggma

FEAR may come knocking
at your door someday. For
Heaven's sake, don't let it
in. Instead, Invite your
Hopes and Dreams in
for a nice long chat.

–WLA
ggma

WE LIVE in the Present.
WE DREAM of the Future.
WE LEARN from the
Lessons of Our Past.

—WLA
ggma

TODAY IS THE DAY!
Surprise Someone with
a Special Kindness plus
FINISH that long overdue
Project. Get excited about
the GOOD THINGS IN LIFE.

–WLA
ggma

"Hate Corrodes, Contaminates
and Changes Everything
it Touches." -From R.J.A.
LET COMPASSION AND HOPE
PROTECT YOU FROM IT.

These are some of the
Best Days of Your Life.
Why waste Time wishing
you were older/younger,
thinner, richer or
somewhere else? Time
goes by so quickly.
ENJOY EVERY MINUTE.

–WLA
ggma

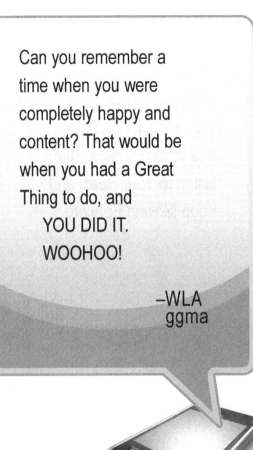

Can you remember a time when you were completely happy and content? That would be when you had a Great Thing to do, and
YOU DID IT.
WOOHOO!

—WLA
ggma

Where are you going
today, tomorrow, next year?
YOU MUST HAVE A PLAN.
(Make sure it is Flexible.)
Listen to Your Heart and
Keep Moving Forward.

–WLA
ggma

Instead of building
High Walls and Fences
for Protection, BUILD
A STRONG NETWORK
OF FAITH, FAMILY AND
FRIENDS to Help Each
Other when needed most.

–WLA
ggma

_____

_____

_____

HOPES AND DREAMS
come with unlimited
refills. You can have
as many as you want
and you can take
them with you
WHEREVER YOU GO.

–WLA
ggma

A WINNER has the
Determination and
Endurance to Reach
the Finish Line. You
don't have to be
First to be a Winner.
FINISHING IS
WINNING!

−WLA
ggma

Watch the Sunrise.
Chase away Clouds.
Smell all the Flowers.
Laugh Out Loud.
Listen to Your Heart
so Brave and Strong
and YOUR LIFE WILL
SING A SWEET SONG.

–WLA
ggma

Some People fail to see
the SILVER LINING in
their Dark Clouds because
they are only looking
FOR THE GOLD.

–WLA
ggma

_____

_____

_____

You may have a lot of
"Busyness" to take care
of today, but Wait a
Minute. Close Your Eyes.
Think of One Thing you
are Grateful for. SWEET!

–WLA
ggma

"We have met the enemy
and they is US."
-Pogo Cartoon
Don't become Your Own
Worst Enemy, Be Your
Own Best Friend.
BELIEVE IN YOURSELF.

–WLA
ggma

_____

_____

_____

The REWARDS of Your TOMORROWS are rooted in the DRUDGERY OF TODAY.

—WLA
ggma

YOU have so many Good Qualities and Outstanding Abilities. Don't hide them. People want to SEE THEM and BE INSPIRED BY THEM.

–WLA ggma

_____

_____

_____

It doesn't take a huge
event to alter the Course
Of Your Life. ONE SMALL
CHANGE can Transform
old bad habits into
NEW GOOD HABITS.

–WLA
ggma

Every Day is a New Beginning with Endless Possibilities. START by doing a Good Deed. It could Be Exciting and Fun. You won't know until
YOU TRY IT ! !

–WLA
ggma

Your Creative Imagination
is one of the Greatest
Talents you have. The
More YOU USE IT, the
Better it gets, and IT
NEVER WEARS OUT.

–WLA
ggma

DISCOVER the Magic of
LIFE though Knowledge
SEE the Promise and
Beauty of LIFE through
NATURE. KNOW the
Real JOY OF LIFE through
LOVING KINDNESS.

–WLA
ggma

One Thing is the same for
the whole Human Race.
WE ALL make mistakes and
Desire to be FORGIVEN,
LOVED AND HELD IN
   HIGH ESTEEM.

–WLA
ggma

_____

_____

_____

A TRUE FRIEND
Helps us THINK
our Best Thoughts;
DO Our Noblest Deeds
and Encourages Us
TO BE OUR BEST SELF.

–WLA
ggma

Consider the postage stamp. It sticks to one thing until it reaches the place it should be. Stay focused on Your Goals. YOU WILL MAKE IT.

–WLA ggma

When everything seems
to be getting on your
"last nerve" Try singing
your favorite song.
SING IT LOUD! Soon
You will feel much better.

–WLA
ggma

A Good Education can
LIFT US UP, out of our
Basic Nature, to Become
GREATER then we ever
Imagined. Remember
the Important Lessons
You have Learned so far.

–WLA
ggma

Everyone should have
Someone who will stand
by them no matter what.
Maybe you can't see me
but I'm here, LOVING YOU
and BELIEVING IN YOU
ALL THE WAY.

–WLA
ggma

People notice when you have Integrity. ACTIONS SPEAK LOUDER THAN WORDS. Always Stand Up for what is RIGHT. You won't be sorry.

–WLA
ggma

If You Listen carefully,
You will hear Opportunity
Knocking on your Heart's
Door. Welcome it in.
LOOK it over and DO
Something With it!

—WLA
ggma

There are many more
Good Times than Bad.
So when Bad Times
come, remember, soon
You will be singing,
"Happy Days are here
again." Trust Me.
   I've Been There.

–WLA
ggma

The Rain is gone;
It's a bright sunny day.
Everyone should go
Outside to play.
Take a deep breath.
Give a Big Shout.
Let all the stress
And pressure out.
Run 'til your legs
won't run any more.
Laugh out Loud 'til
Your sides are sore.
Make a New Plan.
Find a New Way to
Cherish each other
More every day.

FAMILY: We laugh and cry; Share Joy and Pain. And Like ripples on a Pond, when something happens
TO ONE OF US,
IT TOUCHES
ALL OF US.

—WLA ggma

Obstacles and Roadblocks
are what YOU SEE when
you take your Eyes Off
Your Goals. Concentrate
ON YOUR PLANS. Stay
Focused and Enjoy Them.

–WLA
ggma

Failure lies hidden along
the Path of Least Endeavor.
Success takes Time and a
lot of Hard Work but has
Huge Rewards and
NO REGRETS.

–WLA
ggma

It is Time for R. A. O. K.
(Random Acts Of
Kindness.) Reach Out
and do something
"Extra Special" for
Someone today.

–WLA
ggma

Happiness is never far
away. It's in the things
You Do and Say. Start
each day with a Smile
On Your Face, and
Make Your World
A Better Place.

–WLA
ggma

Today will be a Better Day
Because of You.
Your Concern will remind
Someone they are Loved
and Your Smile will give
them the Courage to
Carry On.

—WLA
ggma

YOU can Build a Better World
by improving the people in it.
START WITH YOU!
Learn, Work, Strive to
Become Your Best Self.
Then You can Help Others.

—WLA
ggma

Don't be afraid of Pressure
in Your Daily Life. Deep in
the Earth, Pressure Changes
Rocks into Diamonds.
BE STRONG.
YOU ARE A DIAMOND
IN PROCESS.

–WLA
ggma

For a Happy Rewarding Life
INSPIRE Compassion and
Understanding; SHARE the
Beauty and Promise of
Nature; RADIATE Integrity
and Self-Control.

–WLA
ggma

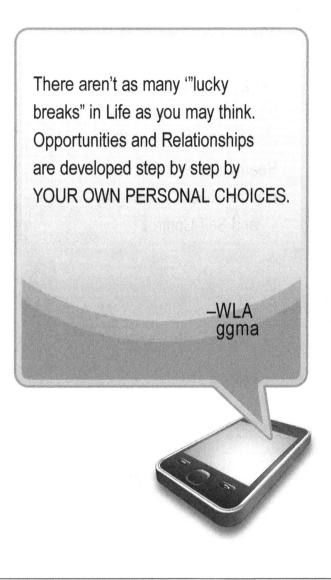

There aren't as many '"lucky breaks" in Life as you may think. Opportunities and Relationships are developed step by step by YOUR OWN PERSONAL CHOICES.

–WLA
ggma

_____

_____

_____

When you get discouraged
with yourself, remember,
Every Saint has a Past and
Every Sinner has a Future.
Your tomorrows will be Better
If You Make Good Plans Today.

—WLA
ggma

If Your Goal in Life is to be
Great in the Eyes of the World,
You may be disappointed. BE
GOOD, BE SMART, BE KIND
AND YOU WILL BE AMONG
THE GREATEST.

–WLA
ggma

The Happiest People on Earth don't have the Best of Everything. They Learn to Make the Most of Everything They Have.

–WLA ggma

LOVE can't be measured
in dollars and cents. Even
a Promise cannot be spent.
Words of Praise are worth
more than Gold and
Increase in Value the
More They Are Told.

–WLA
ggma

Let's talk about our
Dreams and Things
We like to do. We'll
call it "HAPPY TALK."
We need to take time
for Happy Talk. IT IS
A GOOD THING.

—WLA
ggma

Don't be in such a hurry
for Tomorrow that you
miss the Real Joy of Today.
It's Totally Awesome to be
Young, Gorgeous and
Smart Too. ENJOY IT.

–WLA
ggma

Problems are like Workouts. Working Hard to Find the RIGHT Solutions makes You Stronger and Wiser about Yourself And Your Future. KEEP WORKING!

–WLA
ggma

Shhhh! Listen. Do You hear it? It's your Heart whispering, "Somebody Loves You and wants You to Be Happy and Blessed Forever." (That Somebody Is Me.)

–WLA
ggma

KNOWLEDGE, NOT MONEY, IS POWER. The more Knowledge you have, the more Power you have to Make Right Decisions and DO GOOD WORKS that Improve The World.

—WLA
ggma

If YOU were a Race Horse,
I'd Bet On You and Stand
Up and Cheer so the
Whole World Could Hear that
YOU ARE A REAL CHAMPION
EVERY DAY OF THE YEAR.

–WLA
ggma

_____

_____

_____

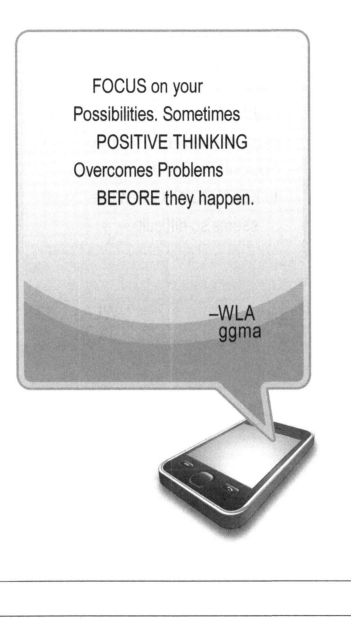

Your Friendly Smile and
Caring Ways are Inspiring.
Someone may be Watching
You and Finding the Courage
to KEEP GOING when Life
seems so difficult.

–WLA
ggma

Let's be multi-lingual
today and SMILE in
every Language we can
think of. Here's my Smile
in Spanish, or French or
Japanese or..... GET IT?

–WLA
ggma

_____

_____

_____

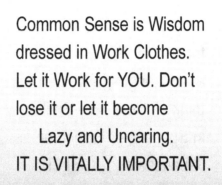

Common Sense is Wisdom
dressed in Work Clothes.
Let it Work for YOU. Don't
lose it or let it become
    Lazy and Uncaring.
IT IS VITALLY IMPORTANT.

–WLA
ggma

_____

_____

_____

There are NO Shortcuts in doing a Good Job. There are many REWARDS in doing Something YOU CAN BE PROUD OF TODAY and Throughout the Coming Years.

–WLA
ggma

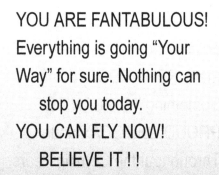

From B.A.I.
"I am a Great Believer
   in Luck.
The harder I Work,
the More I have of it."
    -Thomas Jefferson
  Keep Trying,
  Searching
  and Working,
YOU WILL SUCCEED.

Whazzup Handsome Dude?
(or Gorgeous Girl)
What great mystery will you
solve today? Perhaps you
will Discover that being
Helpful and Kind Creates
a "Domino Effect."

–WLA
ggma

_____

_____

_____

GOOD THINGS still come
to those who wait. There is
a Proper Time for Everything
and so many Spectacular
Adventures are waiting for you.
YOU'LL SEE!

–WLA
ggma

SUCCESS is not Instantaneous. You are NOT Born with it and You can't get it by accident. It takes a lot of Hard Work and Determination to Achieve It.

–WLA
ggma

Old Friends are Gold.
New Friends are Diamonds.
Bring them Together
The New and the Old.
Diamonds are Lovely
Surrounded by Gold.

–WLA
ggma

Not ALL who "Wander"
through Life are LOST.
Sooner or Later, the
Right Path will appear.
Often times, Sooner
would be Better, but
IT IS NEVER TOO LATE !

–WLA
ggma

YOU can make a difference.
   One Kind Word;
   One Good Deed;
   One Person At A Time.

                          –WLA
                          ggma

_____

_____

_____

Don't be afraid to REINVENT Yourself. If what you were yesterday isn't working for you today, DECIDE what you Should DO TO FIX IT, THEN DO IT WITH ALL YOUR HEART.

—WLA ggma

The Best Way to
Improve Yourself is from
the Inside-Out. Are you a
Positive Thinker?
REAL CHANGE IS
AN INSIDE JOB.

–WLA
ggma

To Those who SEE
   with Loving Eyes,
   Life is Beautiful.
To Those who SEE
   with Loathing Eyes,
   Life is Miserable.
YOUR EYES.
YOUR CHOICE.

–WLA
ggma

_____

_____

_____

KINDNESS IS FREE and yet
it makes everyone RICHER;
those Who Receive it and
Those Who Give it. Now
isn't that remarkable?.

−WLA
ggma

_____

_____

_____

Your Thoughts are
the Architects of Your
Destiny. What are
THEY BUILDING
FOR YOU TODAY?

–WLA
ggma

Paganini, the Great Violinist said, "The Music is not in the instrument, it is in My Soul." THE MUSIC OF YOUR LIFE IS IN YOUR SOUL. PLAY ON!

–WLA ggma

PERFECTION may not
always be attainable,
but if you AIM for it,
you may Achieve
  EXCELLENCE,
  and that is
  ABOVE AVERAGE,
  SUPERIOR AND
  EXTRAORDINARY !

                    −WLA
                    ggma

_____

_____

_____

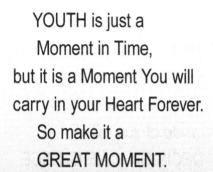

YOUTH is just a
Moment in Time,
but it is a Moment You will
carry in your Heart Forever.
So make it a
GREAT MOMENT.

–WLA
ggma

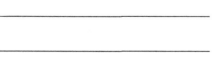

Integrity and Credibility
are not automatically
included in your DNA.
They are formed deep
inside of you - ONE
DECISION, ONE CHOICE
AT A TIME.

–WLA
ggma

Very often, I find
Thoughts of You
come to mind,
And My Heart enjoys
a Bright Happy Minute
Full of Hopes and
Prayers For You in it.

—WLA
ggma

An Important Lesson
to Learn in Life is
Self-Discipline; the
regulation of Thought
and Action pertaining
to PROPER CONDUCT.

–WLA
ggma

"The Essence of Genius
that dazzles mortal Eyes
is often PERSEVERANCE
in disguise."
-Henry Austin

–WLA
ggma

The ONE who Dares to
TRY the most, WINS
the Most. It is the law of
averages. The more you
Try, the more chances
For Winning.

–WLA
ggma

TRUTH is Interesting and Exciting and sometimes Stranger than Fiction. But it is Never as Strange as Lies.

—WLAggma

There is No such thing
as "can't" - only "won't."
Just like the little Ant,
You have to have
High Hopes.
Don't Doubt Yourself.
YOU CAN DO IT!

—WLA
ggma

A Great Leader does
Not promote his own
importance. He
INSPIRES OTHERS
to have confidence in
Their Own Abilities.

–WLA
ggma

There is Victory in Sports and
Battle and also in daily Life.
To Conquer what you once
thought was impossible is a
VICTORY. THAT CAN
HAPPEN EVERY DAY.

–WLA
ggma

Make it a daily habit to be
Thankful for what You Have
rather than complain about
what You Don't Have.
Honestly, Life is just
easier that way.

–WLA
ggma

No matter how Bad you think your Life is: LOOK AROUND! There are many people whose Lives are much worse. So You really Do Have many reasons To Be Grateful.

–WLA
ggma

When the night seems
lonely and dark,
Dreams can take you
Away to Play
Among the Stars.
When you awake,
You may find,
Left behind,
Some Stardust
In Your Eyes.

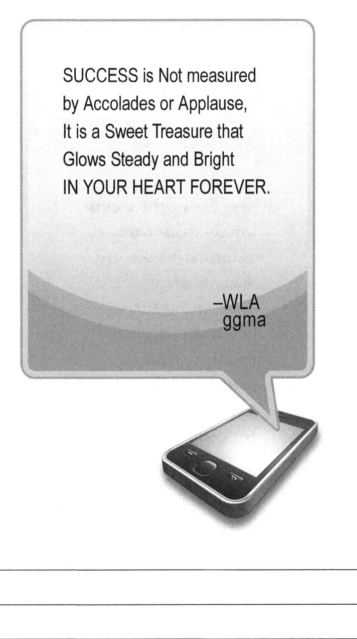

SUCCESS is Not measured
by Accolades or Applause,
It is a Sweet Treasure that
Glows Steady and Bright
IN YOUR HEART FOREVER.

–WLA
ggma

A circle of Blessing is
made of Gratitude,
Trust, Forgiveness and
a LOVING HEART that
knows what to remember
and what to forget.

–WLA
ggma

From K.J.
"I slept and dreamed that Life was Joy. I awoke and saw that Life was Service. I acted and Behold, SERVICE WAS JOY."
 - *Robindranath Tagore*

–WLA
ggma

Constant self-criticism
eats away your self-esteem.
Don't make a habit of it.
Recognize your many
outstanding qualities
and BE GRATEFUL.

–WLA
ggma

There is significant Growth in Moral Character when Respect and Concern for Others become a Primary Motivation in your LIFE.

–WLA ggma

Your Beautiful Smile is
a Welcoming Light shining
from the window of Your
Soul so Everyone can see
that Your Heart is at Home.

–WLA
ggma

If you WANT Your Dreams
to come true, WAKE UP!
GET UP! GET OUT THERE
and find a way to MAKE
THEM ALL COME TRUE.

–WLA
ggma

Some days you feel
like you're on Top Of
The World. Other days
you may feel like you're
in a Deep Valley.
KEEP LOOKING UP!
You'll be back on
TOP again soon.

–WLA
ggma

Square your shoulders.
Hold Your Head High.
Walk With Confidence.
Be Happy and Proud
of Who You Are Today
and Every Day.
YOU ARE MAGNIFICENT!

—WLA
ggma

At Every Age,
LIFE Requires a
lot of PATIENCE....
and COURAGE....
and HOPE....
and....
(You fill in that blank.)

–WLA
ggma

The Way to Begin a long
Journey is to take that
First Step. The Secret
to "getting ahead" is
making a Good Start.
IT'S NEVER
TOO LATE
TO START.

–WLA
ggma

True Happiness is
   "HOME MADE."
You can't buy it, even
   at the most expensive
stores or get it from anyone
on Earth. THE RECIPE IS
   INSIDE YOUR HEART.

                    –WLA
                    ggma

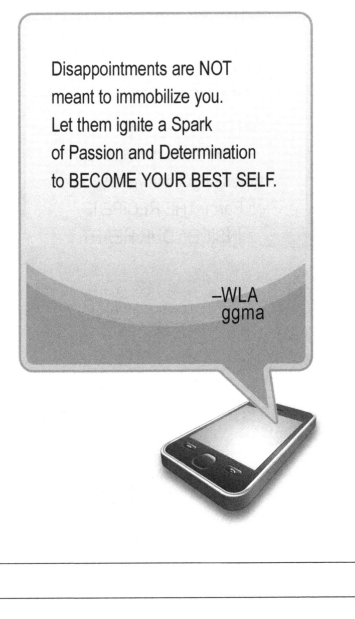

Your True Character is
revealed in what you Say
and Do when it feels like
no one cares about you.
IT IS IMPORTANT TO
MAINTAIN YOUR DIGNITY.

–WLA
ggma

An enemy in Your Head
takes up more space than
a Friend in your Heart. May
you have a Heart Full of
GOOD FRIENDS AND
   NO SPACE
   FOR ENEMIES.

                        –WLA
                         ggma

Good Morning
Miss Gorgeous Girl,
(Mr. Handsome Guy.)
Here is another day Full
of Adventure and Opportunity.
IT'S FREE. IT'S BEAUTIFUL.
IT'S YOURS. ENJOY IT!

–WLA
ggma

_____

_____

_____

Vision without Action is a
Daydream. Action without
Vision is a Nightmare.
    MAKE A PLAN!
Then, step by step,
    Work Toward
    Your Goals.

–WLA
ggma

Today is a good day for
Reflection. What have
you accomplished so
far this year? What do
you want to do in the
days ahead? In twenty
years or so, these will
be "Your Good Ole Days."

No One who really
Concentrates on doing
the RIGHT THING ever
loses his Self-Respect
or the Respect of Others
(even though it may be
unspoken.)

–WLA
ggma

Do Whatever Good you can
do with what you have,
wherever you are. Don't be
afraid to be Helpful and
Kind. It is the Most
Rewarding Thing
You Can Do.

–WLA
ggma

Adopt the pace of Nature.
Her Secret is Patience.
Even the most beautiful
flower is in the shadows
at times. HOLD ON.
HERE COMES THE SUN.

–WLA
ggma

Being Humble does NOT mean "Lacks Confidence." It means "Lacks Arrogance."

—WLA ggma

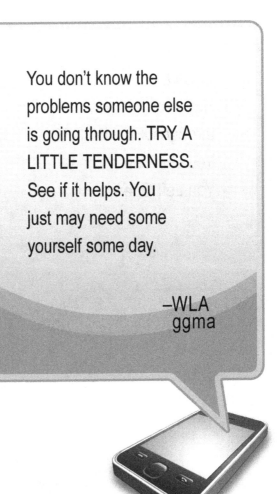

BEWARE of the loud voice
that defends a weak position.
Calmly examine all of the
evidence. Let Your
 CONSCIENCE
 BE YOUR GUIDE.

–WLA
ggma

There is magic in
being Thankful. It is
the Language of Love.
Thank someone for
LOVING YOU TODAY.
I Love You. Thank You
For Loving Me.

–WLA
ggma

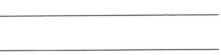

_____

_____

_____

"Sharing" Your
Gratitude brings a
Double Blessing.
The more THANKS
You Give, the more
Real Joy You
Will Receive.

–WLA
ggma

The people who
Know Real Success
are those who are
Cheerful, Hopeful and
Helpful and who take
care of business with
a Smile and a
A Grateful Heart.

–WLA
ggma

You were created to
make a difference in
this World. HOW may
not be clear to you
right now. It will be
some day. YOU ARE
IMPORTANT TODAY
AND EVERY DAY.

—WLA
ggma

You have Beautiful
Music inside of you
just waiting to be
heard. Go ahead.
   SING OUT!
Fill the World with your
Own Incredible Song.
   They Will Love It.

                    –WLA
                     ggma

How do you BUILD
Confidence? By
Completing Smaller
Tasks, on your way
to Larger Tasks.

–WLA
ggma

Your Perspective is
how you CHOOSE
to See Things and
becomes Your Own
REALITY. When you
Develop a Good Positive
Attitude. YOU WILL BE
A HAPPY PERSON.

–WLA
ggma

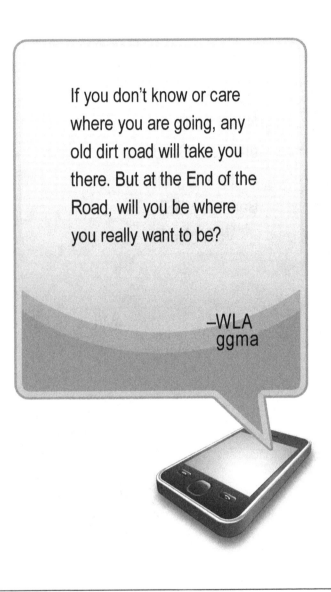

If you don't know or care where you are going, any old dirt road will take you there. But at the End of the Road, will you be where you really want to be?

–WLA
ggma

WARNING: The World is full of Over Stimulation, which may cause you to lose your sense of direction. Don't be distracted. Keep Your Eyes On Your Goals.

–WLA
ggma

Everyone wants to be
Needed. Everyone
Needs to be Wanted.
Today, "Show and Tell"
someone how very much
you Appreciate them.
Aw, come on. DO IT!

—WLA
ggma

Some cloudy days are like
onions. Every layer you
peel away makes you cry.
DRY THOSE TEARS.
Soon, the Sun Will Come
Out and Your Heart
Will Smile Again.

—WLA
ggma

WAKE UP. GET UP!
Put a Smile on your Face
for the whole Human Race.
Do Your Happy Dance!
WOW. YOU ROCK!
It's going to be a
Great Day.

–WLA
ggma

External circumstances
do Not determine the
inner Quality of Your Life.
How YOU CHOOSE to
Respond to them will
Impact Your Life and
Establish Your Path.

–WLA
ggma

The World is NOT searching for "Great" Men and Women. They want Ordinary People who SEE the NEED and are Willing to STEP UP AND DO GREAT THINGS!

–WLA
ggma

Sometimes, it is the very Things you THINK YOU KNOW, that keep you from LEARNING the things YOU SHOULD KNOW.

–WLA ggma

Seasons change at the
Right Time. Flowers and
Trees Grow just as they
should. Animals and Birds
Thrive without our input.
A Higher Power takes
care of it all, and WILL
TAKE CARE OF YOU TOO.

Deep in your Heart you
Know what's good and bad,
wrong and right. You
Learned it from the start.
CHERISH THE TEACHING
AND THE TEACHER.
THEY ARE PRICELESS

–WLA
ggma

There are 525,000 minutes (8,936 hours) in the year ahead just waiting for ALL YOUR UNIQUE, INNOVATIVE AND HELPFUL IDEAS.

–WLA
ggma

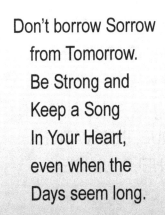

Don't borrow Sorrow
from Tomorrow.
Be Strong and
Keep a Song
In Your Heart,
even when the
Days seem long.

–WLA
ggma

Offer your Words as
Gifts so when they
are unwrapped they
will be uplifting,
bringing Comfort
and Goodwill.

–WLA
ggma

EVERY DAY, You are writing a little more of your own History. These Days will soon be Your Memories. Make sure they are worth Remembering Again.

—WLA
ggma

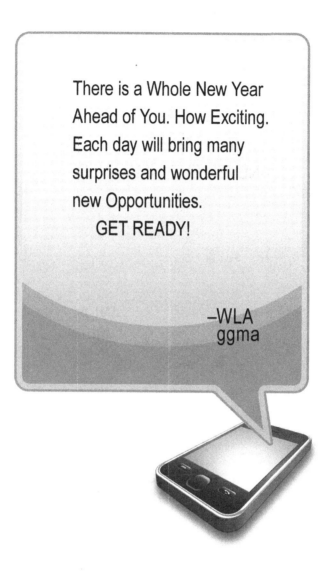

"IF You Use the Abilities you have been given Wisely. more will be given to you until you have an ABUNDANCE."

—WLA ggma

Even if the walls
of your house are
thin, may they be
Strong enough to
keep HATE OUT
and HOLD LOVE IN.

—WLA
ggma

HOME is where
YOUR STORY
BEGINS WITH
LOVE. And That
Love will go with
You wherever you
go and will Keep
You Warm when
the nights are cold.

–WLA
ggma

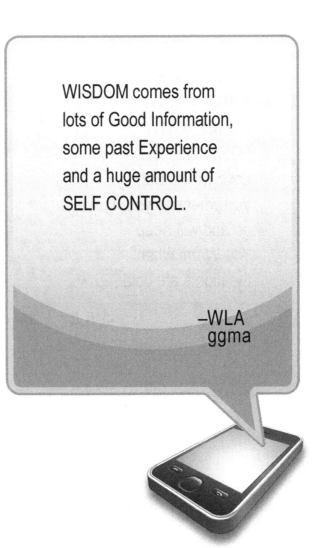

WISDOM comes from
lots of Good Information,
some past Experience
and a huge amount of
SELF CONTROL.

–WLA
ggma

PLEASE ENJOY A
GOOD NEW YEAR
FILLED WITH LOTS OF
GOOD NEWS,
GOOD FORTUNE,
GOOD HEALTH
AND JUST ENOUGH
WEALTH TO DO
GOOD DEEDS AND
LIVE A GOOD LIFE. –WLA
ggma

Always Remember,
You Are Braver than
You Believe you are;
Stronger than
You Seem to be;
Smarter than
You Think you are;
And Twice as Beautiful
As You Ever Imagined
You Could Be.

Sincere Love and Appreciation to:

Andrew & Brennan	Jenn D.
Aaron	Joshua
Alice	Kathie J.
Allan	Kathy G.
Amy	Katie C.
Angie	Katie M.
Annie	Katie N.
Barbara	Lauren N.
Ben	Mary & Dan
Brittany	Michelle
Caesar	Melanie
Caleb	Milo
Carla	Paige
Carolyn & Family	Pam
Chris	Patricia & Family
Christy	Rachelle
Clark	Randy
Connor	Seth
Cory	Steve J.
Darla & Family	Steven
Dorothy	Terri
Eileen	Theron
Enrique	Tom
Gina & Family	Trevor
Ian	Vicki & Family
Iris	Zoey
Jacob	

Printed in the United States
By Bookmasters